DEVELOPING PROGRESSIVE WEB APPLICATIONS WITH ANGULAR (AND IONIC)

How to Build and Deploy Mobile Applications
without Paying Apple or Google for the Privilege

Michael D. Callaghan

Table of Contents

Michael Callaghan

Michael Callaghan

Michael Callaghan

Preface

As a software developer, you want your apps to reach as many people as possible, right? But everyone uses a different platform: Android, iOS, desktop, web. It can be frustrating. Which platform should you target to reach the most users possible? How about all of them! Progressive Web Apps, or PWAs, let you do just that.

Throughout this book, I'll show you how to get a Progressive Web Application off the ground with Angular and Ionic, which will make it easy for you to target the web, iOS, Android, and even desktop apps if you want.

By the end of this book, you should have all the knowledge and confidence you need to stand up a PWA that all your potential users can enjoy.

Who Should Read This Book?

I wrote this book primarily for experienced web developers, who need an extra bit of information to get their Angular apps out of the App Stores and into the hands of users.

Before you begin, I am going to assume you have the following:

Web Development experience.

A working understanding of HTML.

Experience with JavaScript or TypeScript will be helpful.

I am also assuming that you already have an Angular app that you want to host as a PWA. If you have already used Ionic, that will be helpful. I will not use much Ionic, because that is not what this book is about. But the sample app and some of the minor modifications I will make use the Ionic Framework for its UI.

Michael Callaghan

Introduction to Progressive Web Applications

What is a Progressive Web App, and why should you care? You probably already have some idea, or you would not be reading this book. However, humor me a moment.

An often-overlooked topic when discussing a new technology is "why should you care?" This is especially important in an enterprise environment because the introduction of new things typically involves some level of risk.

New and shiny things are cool. Unfortunately, that is not enough of a reason to adopt a new technology. Fortunately, there is more to PWAs than just being the latest and greatest thing.

One of my favorite reasons to choose a PWA is that there are no app store submissions. If you are building an app for the enterprise, you may not want it distributed to users outside of your organization.

With a PWA, users install your app through a simple URL. There are other enterprise solutions for distributing internal apps, but they are often costly and sometimes more complicated than using Apple's or Google's submission process.

Also, by not submitting to an app store, you cannot have a faceless stranger reject your app. I actually had an app rejected by Apple because, "it provided no user value." Ouch.

Another benefit is that updating a PWA is no different than updating any other web app. Your features or bug fixes can go live as quickly as your build process allows. With a PWA, you can truly target multiple platforms with a single codebase. Because a good PWA is responsive, it should look good and function well on any device: desktop, phone, or tablet. In fact, if you think about these things, PWAs help to *reduce* risk.

Michael Callaghan

What Makes a Good PWA?

Google's explanation of a Progressive Web App consists of a few core concepts.

- A PWA should be reliable. It should hold up under difficult network conditions, including slow or even no network connectivity at all.

- It should be fast-- assets such as images should be lazy loaded, and then cached on the user's device, resulting in a short load time.

- PWAs should be engaging, meaning that they should look and behave just like a native app. That includes the ability to install the app on a mobile device's home screen.

- And as the name implies, a Progressive Web App should be progressive. In other words, it should take advantage of modern features when available, and gracefully degrade, while still providing a seamless user experience.

These are just some of the concepts you will want to keep in mind as you progress through the book.

If you would like a sneak peek, Google has a more detailed checklist at its PWA site for developers, at https://web.dev/pwa-checklist/.

Google Lighthouse

Google provides an automated tool called Lighthouse to help ensure that a web app meets everything in that checklist. Lighthouse will analyze your app and provide a PWA score between 0, meaning you have accomplished nothing, through a perfect score of 100. It also helpfully provides suggestions on what you can do to improve your score, such as…

- Ensuring your app is served securely over HTTPS.

Michael Callaghan

- Adding service workers.

- Improving page load times.

- Including a web manifest and other assets to enable installation to a mobile device's home screen.

- You will use Lighthouse to score our own app later.

Popular Progressive Web Apps

Before you move on, here are some popular PWAs, which you can use today, and see how great the experience can be.

Michael Callaghan

Twitter

Twitter's PWA is practically identical to its native app. Its Lighthouse score is only 65, which means it does not implement every PWA feature perfectly. That said, it is still a great experience, and a fine example of what can be accomplished with a PWA.

Michael Callaghan

Instagram

Instagram has a PWA that scores about as well as Twitter's, primarily because it still prompts the user to install their native app and does not include a splash screen. Its performance, however, is exceptional.

Michael Callaghan

Starbucks

Starbucks decided to create and test a PWA version of their mobile app. The result is an application that achieved a perfect Lighthouse score, and whose code size is 99% smaller than their native iOS version. It is fast and responsive, with smooth animations and a native appearance.

Michael Callaghan

Uber

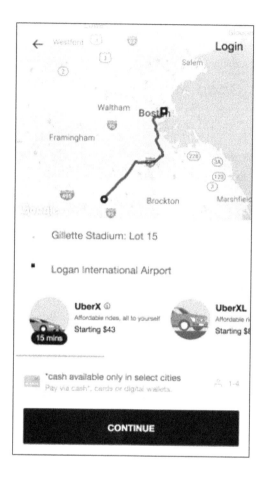

Likewise, Uber's PWA is a fantastic app, and achieved a perfect Lighthouse score. It correctly selected my address when I experimented with it. You can use it to summon a ride, without ever having to install their native app.

What all these PWAs have in common is that they are fast, easily installable, and look fantastic. They are everything you should shoot for when constructing your own PWA.

Michael Callaghan

Which brings me to a topic I am sure you have been wondering about… What exactly caused me to investigate PWAs in the first place?

Michael Callaghan

My PWA Journey

First, I do not have a company like Starbucks or Uber. So please allow me to explain what happened to me, and why I became so captivated with PWAs.

Deploying to app stores is painful. It is hard. There are many aspects of deploying apps that you must get right, and the process differs between the Apple App Store and the Google Play Store. Here are some of the things you need to do.

To build and deploy an app, you need to understand and complete the following steps:

- You need to have the proper Developer Account. Apple charges $99/year for an individual. Google is a much more reasonable $25 one time.
- You must understand, create, and install device profiles for the devices you intend to support.
- You must create and install the proper Signing certificates. These are used to encode your app cryptographically and prove that you are the one who created it.
- You need to decide what devices you intend to support.
- Of course, you need to design, code, and build your app.
- Then you must sign your app with the signing certificates created earlier.
- Next, you bundle the app, and upload it to each store.

Michael Callaghan

If you think you are done at this point, you are not. Before you can make your app available to the public, there are other assets you need to provide:

- You will need to supply marketing videos and screenshots of the application at various resolutions for a variety of device types and sizes.
- You need to create icons at multiple resolutions.
- You will have to complete a questionnaire to determine the right age rating.
- You need to set a price. Note that if you set your app to Free on Google Play, you can never charge for it.
- You must create and supply a Privacy Policy.

Once you have done all this, only then can you submit your app for review. And then you wait. In the past, this process could take weeks. Though it has gotten faster, you do not control it. If you did not get everything right above, and sometimes even if you did, you may have your application rejected. That is what happened to me. Both Apple and Google rejected my application outright, and was the final straw motivating me to release my app as a PWA.

The Offending Application

What was this horrific application, you ask? It all starts with Mario Kart 8 for the Nintendo Wii U.

Michael Callaghan

My family loves playing Mario Kart. No, I did not create a Mario Kart 8 clone for mobile phones. I created a utility my children and I could use *while we play* Mario Kart.

After a few years playing this amazing game, every member of my family had a favorite character, car, wheel, and wing combination. This led to many evenings of predictable outcomes. One night, my youngest child suggested that we randomly select our combinations.

We started by rolling dice, until one day, another child asked whether I could create an app that does the same thing. I spent the weekend and came up with this: An Ionic-Angular app, complete with 3D animations and sound effects, which could be deployed to either iPhones or Androids.

Michael Callaghan

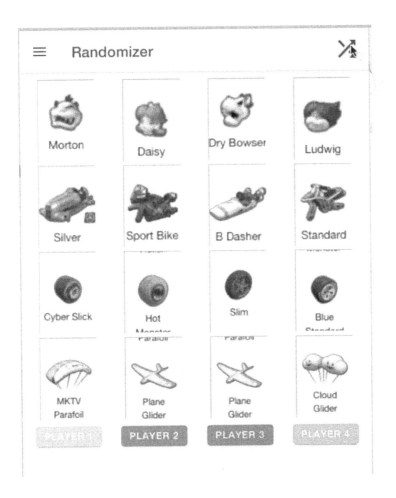

Please keep in mind there are other utilities on both stores that assist with playing Mario Kart, so I assumed I would be safe. I was sadly mistaken. My rejection from Apple was swift, (pun intended) and brief. It simply said, "Your app or its metadata appears to contain misleading content. Specifically, your app creates a misleading association with Mario Kart." My home page clearly indicates that I am not affiliated with Nintendo in any way.

Google's rejection was even shorter: "Your application has been suspended."

Michael Callaghan

I appealed both rejections, explaining why I thought it should be allowed. Apple disagreed. Google never responded.

It was then I discovered how easy it would be to turn the application into a PWA and let others experience the joy thus far denied to them.

Getting the App

My goal in writing this book is to demonstrate how to deploy an existing application as a PWA. To that end, I am offering you a choice: You may use your own app, or if you do not have one, you may use mine. The only requirement is that it be an Angular app, preferably Angular 8 or later.

To use mine, you will need to clone my GitHub repo, which you can download from https://github.com/walkingriver/mk8r-pwa. If you prefer the direct approach, you can clone the repo using either of the following commands:

```
git clone git@github.com:walkingriver/mk8r-pwa.git
git clone https://github.com/walkingriver/mk8r-pwa.git
```

This repo has multiple branches representing various stages of development. To follow along, start at the master branch.

Viewing the App

Now that you have the project; you can quickly fire up the application in a browser and see what you get out of the box.

If you have not already done so, open a command terminal and enter the project folder.

Next, enter the command

```
npm install
```

Michael Callaghan

This will download and install the node dependencies of this application so that you can run it locally. Once that command has completed, run

```
ng serve
```

This builds the project into a working application and creates a temporary web server that will let you see the application in a browser. It will also watch for changes to your source code, and automatically rebuild and reload the application.

After a bunch of log messages, mostly from the angular CLI, the application is ready. Your system's default web browser should open and show the home page of the app. If it does not, open a browser to http://localhost:4200.

Play around with the application for a few minutes. In the next chapter, you will upload it to a web server to make it visible to the world.

Michael Callaghan

Hosting the App

All web apps need to be hosted somewhere, and PWAs are no exception. Now that you have your application running, you need to find a place to host it and see how it scores as a PWA. I have chosen Firebase to host the application. This chapter will provide a quick overview and help you get it deployed.

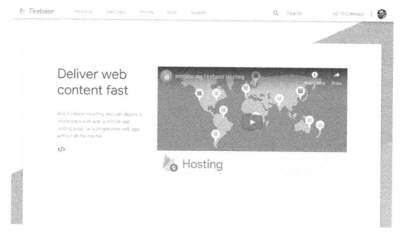

Firebase is an extremely popular cloud platform from Google. There are dozens of features that it supports, from authentication to globally replicated databases, to machine learning. You are going to be using it to host your PWA.

Many people use and recommended hosting your apps with Firebase, and there are some solid reasons:

- First, it is dead simple to deploy your app. All it takes is a single command.

- PWAs are required to be loaded securely. Firebase provides free SSL certificates automatically.

- With Firebase, all your content is hosted on fast SSDs and served from CDNs all over the world.

Michael Callaghan

- Best of all, you can start without spending any money.

Firebase Quick Start

The first thing you will do is use the Firebase console to create a hosting project for the app. Then you will create a production build. You will add some firebase specific settings to the app. You will need to connect your local app to your firebase hosting project. Finally, you will make sure it works locally.

First, head to https://console.firebase.google.com/ and log in with your Google account, which is required. If you do not already have an account, you will be able to create one.

This is my firebase console. Yours will look similar but will be empty if this is your first time using it. This is where you will be creating the project to host the application. Click the Add Project button and follow the steps. Note the name of the Firebase project you create. You will need it soon.

The following table contains the list of commands that you will use to install the firebase tools locally, connect your app, and then build and deploy it.

All but the last two of these commands only need to be performed once.

Command	Description
`npm -g install firebase-tools`	Install the firebase command-line tools.
`firebase login`	Open a browser where you will be prompted to login to your Google account.
`firebase projects:list`	See what projects you have configured in firebase with the command.
`ng build --prod`	Use this command to build a production version of the app, which you need before you can deploy.
`firebase init`	This command will add some configuration so that the firebase CLI knows how your app is configured. It will ask you which firebase project to use. Select the one you just created. It will want to know which folder it should expect to find your build artifacts. By default, in an Angular application, this should be your www folder. It will also ask you whether to overwrite index.html, which you should not.
`firebase use --add`	If you ever want to change the project or add another one, you can issue the firebase use –add command. This will let you set

Michael Callaghan

	up additional deployment slots, such as staging or production.
`firebase serve`	Before you deploy everything up to firebase, you can use this command to ensure that everything is working locally. This is like the ng serve or ionic serve commands, in that a local web server will be spun up for you but using Firebase's tooling instead of Angular's.
`firebase deploy`	Deploys the application to Firebase. You will be presented with a custom URL you can use to launch the application.

Please follow these steps now to deploy the application to Firebase and launch the browser to the custom URL provided.

In the next chapter, you will audit the application and see what you need to do to turn it into a true PWA.

Michael Callaghan

Measuring PWA Performance

Using a framework makes it easy to get a project off the ground quickly, though it may not always provide the most optimized solution possible. As you will see in this chapter, the application I built using the Ionic Framework and Angular scaffolding gets you about halfway there. This is a pretty good start. To remediate the other half, there are some tools and techniques you can use to help measure and improve the performance of our app.

The tool you will be using in this module is Google's Lighthouse, an open source auditing web site auditing tool. Lighthouse will audit the application and show you what you need to fix.

Let us review the results of the audit, showing what the scaffolding provided and the items that still need to be addressed, which Lighthouse calls "opportunities." Finally, I will choose a few of those opportunities to remediate and see how the score changes.

Lighthouse

Lighthouse is Google's open source PWA auditing tool, which you can use to score a web application. Once you have the audit results, you can use that information to make your PWA better.

Michael Callaghan

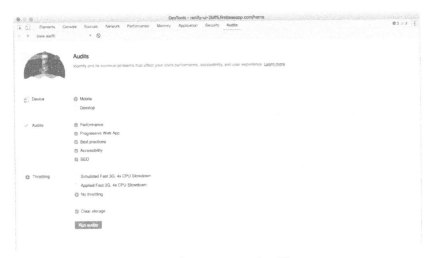

To do this, you simply need to turn on the Chrome DevTools and have it run its audits. Do that now, and then you can review its findings and discuss what they mean.

Open a fresh instance of Chrome and navigate to the URL where the application is deployed. The page should render, and that is OK. Let it run. Open the Chrome DevTools and select the Audits tab. Once there, run all the audits for Mobile, with no network throttling. Then click the blue Run audits button.

Michael Callaghan

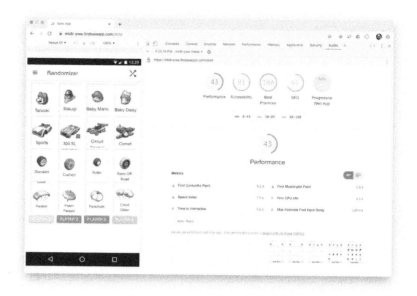

As you can see, the Ionic and Angular tools do a pretty good job. But the worst score is in fact Progressive Web App, so you still have lots of work to do. Scroll down a bit and you can see what that work is.

Michael Callaghan

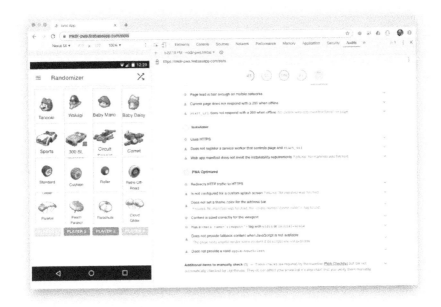

Here are the PWA audit results. Quickly review the ones that passed, and then look at the ones that failed.

Michael Callaghan

Service workers

Before addressing the audit opportunities, I want to take a moment to discuss Service Workers. Progressive Web Applications are built on top of service workers. Thus, any discussion of PWAs would be incomplete without including them. But what is a service worker?

According to Google, a service worker is simply a script that your browser runs in the background, separate from a web page. It's a simple thing, in concept. But a powerful idea that opens the door to all sorts of things.

A service worker acts somewhat like a waiter or waitress for your application, taking your orders and providing the most relevant content, under rules that you control.

Service workers can support offline-first scenarios, by caching often-used and frequently unchanging assets and resources.

Related to that is that your application can require network connectivity but provide default resources that will be loaded in the event of a temporary network error.

Because they work in the background, a service worker can asynchronously download new versions of those assets, and even your application itself, when network conditions permit. This can be done quietly, or with appropriate notifications to the application user.

None of this cool functionality without cost, however. There are some drawbacks. Service Workers only work on pages served over HTTPS. You already knew about that restriction, though, so you're OK there.

Service workers cannot interact directly with your page's document object model. You can still communicate with the page by using the HTML window's `postMessage` interface. Your application can listen for messages from your service worker and take appropriate action.

Michael Callaghan

Not all browsers support service workers yet. That means, in today's progressive web applications, you need to be mindful of the fact that some browsers won't be able to use all these great new features.

Finally, service workers are complex, and not trivial to write.

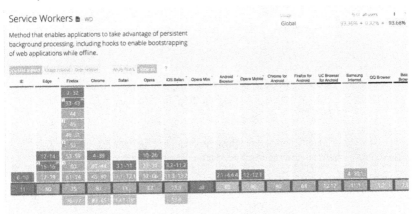

Regarding browser support, before relying on service workers, you should pay a visit to https://caniuse.com and see what the current state of support is. At the time of this writing, no versions of Internet Explorer support them, though the Edge browser has full support since version 17. If you know your users are on Windows, you could gently suggest that they use Edge for the best experience.

All the other desktop browsers seem to offer full support, and even most mobile browsers that are likely to be in use today (again, excluding Internet Explorer).

Keep this in mind as you deploy your PWA, especially in a corporate environment where users are forced to use IE for everything.

This chart represents a high-level timeline of how a service worker works in a typical application.

Michael Callaghan

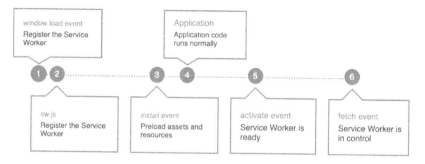

1. When the window has finished loading, some script on your page will register worker, causing it to be loaded and started.

2. The service worker script is loaded and executed

3. And then its install event is fired. The service worker can start pre-fetching and caching certain application assets and resources.

4. At this point, your application runs normally, mostly unaware that the service worker is there.

5. Soon after the activate event is fired, indicating that the service worker can now start handling fetches on behalf of your application.

6. This can be followed by multiple fetch events. Responding to this event, the service worker is in control of just about any resource your application may request. Based on how the service worker is implemented and configured, it can decide whether to allow your application's requests to proceed as normal, or it can respond with a cached version of the requested resource.

Here is the default Google implementation for registering a service worker.

```
if ('serviceWorker' in navigator) {
  window.addEventListener('load', function () {
    navigator.serviceWorker.register('/sw.js')
```

Michael Callaghan

```
        .then(function (registration) {
            // Registration was successful
            console.log('ServiceWorker registration
successful with scope: ', registration.scope);
        }, function (err) {
            // registration failed :(
            console.log('ServiceWorker registration
failed: ', err);
        });
    });
}
```

The first line checks to make sure that serviceWorker is defined. Remember, not all browsers support service workers, and you want your site to work in as many browsers as possible. Assuming the browser supports them, an event listener is added to the window object, responding to the load event. This ensures the page is complete before trying to register the service worker, which happens on the next line. The register function takes as its sole parameter the path to script containing the service worker, in this case a file called sw.js in the web root. It returns a promise, which resolves on successful registration, or rejects with any errors that occur.

At that point, the browser will execute the service worker code inside the sw.js script.

But this is as far as I will ask you to go down this path. This is an introductory book, and while some people like to dive deep into the ins and outs of this stuff, I prefer to let others do the heavy lifting so I can focus on my application code.

Fortunately, there are a few libraries to help you manage these details so that you don't have to. In the next section, I'll introduce you to one of the easiest of those libraries, the Angular PWA package.

Michael Callaghan

Improving Performance with Angular PWA

Angular provides an npm package to make implementing services workers easy, removing most of the boilerplate and complexity you saw earlier. In this chapter, you will use Angular PWA to help fix those audit opportunities. It will do most of the work for you.

There were six issues, or opportunities, that Lighthouse highlighted for you to fix.

1. The application does not respond if there is no network

2. When a PWA is configured properly, the browser can prompt the user to install it. As currently configured, our app doesn't qualify.

3. There is no service worker, which I'm going to defer to the next module

4. There is no content rendered in the page body if JavaScript is disabled. The recommendation is to show the user something, even if it's just something that tells them to turn on JavaScript.

5. You don't have a splash screen, which you'll fix in a few moments.

6. Likewise, you can theme the browser address bar to match the site. You'll take care of that here, too.

The Angular CLI provides a handy way to add PWA capabilities to an existing application, and much like you did with the firebase configuration, it's a single command.

```
npx ng add @angular/pwa
```

Michael Callaghan

The @angular/pwa package added some files to the project and modified others. The new files are:

- A service worker configuration file, which sets up the caching rules for the angular service worker. You'll take a closer look at this file in the next module.

- The web manifest file is processed by the browser that's rendering your app. It provides information about the content and behavior of your application when it's installed by your users on their devices.

- It also added some default icons, which you'll customize later

Service Worker Configuration

The provided service worker configuration file is straightforward, and you won't spend too much time on it. I just want you to see it so that you understand what's happening.

```
"index": "/index.html",
  "assetGroups": [{
    "name": "app",
    "installMode": "prefetch",
    "resources": {
      "files": ["/favicon.ico", "/index.html",
"/*.css", "/*.js"]
    }
  }, {
    "name": "assets",
    "installMode": "lazy",
    "updateMode": "prefetch",
    "resources": {
      "files": ["/assets/**"]
    }
  }
  ]
```

The index property indicates the file that represents the startup page for your application, which will almost always be index.html.

The rest of the file is a single section, assetGroups. Each group contains a name, a set of resources, and fetch/update policy called install mode.

In the app section, its installMode is set to prefetch, which tells the service worker to grab every type of resource listed in the section while it is loading and caching the current version of the application. In this case, the fav icon, index.html page, all css stylesheets, and all javascript files, will be downloaded and cached immediately upon first load.

Whereas prefetch is the default install mode, you can also specify lazy, which is self-explanatory. Lazy tells the service worker not to bother loading and caching these resources until they are needed. In the assets group configuration, every file in any folder underneath the assets folder is lazy loaded. The double-asterisk in the files array means any folder or subfolder, so all folders beneath /assets are affected. The assets group also indicates an updateMode, prefetch. When the service worker detects a new version of the application, it will prefetch all the currently cached assets immediately. Because installMode is set to lazy, you could also specify updateMode to be lazy, which would wait until the assets are needed before loading the new versions.

As you can imagine, your prefetching and caching strategy could get quite complicated.

Here is a snippet of the web app manifest file. The information in this file pertains to the application when installed on a device. The properties are straightforward, and you will be customizing them in the final module of this book.

```
{
  "name": "Mario Kart Randomizer",
  "short_name": "MK8R",
```

Michael Callaghan

```
"theme_color": "#75D0F7",
"background_color": "#fafafa",
"display": "standalone",
"start_url": "/slots",
"scope": "/",
"icons": [
  {
    "src": "assets/icons/manifest-icon-192.png",
    "sizes": "192x192",
    "type": "image/png"
  },
```

For now, it is enough to see the file and know it exists.

Angular provides a default set of icons, which you are free to replace. Essentially, it's the same icon, configured for different device resolutions. These icons are used when the application is installed on a device, and you'll play with them in the final module.

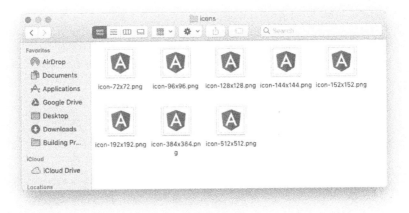

For now, you can leave the Angular logo.

Modified Existing Project Files

It also modified some of the existing project files.

Michael Callaghan

```
"assets": [
  {
    "glob": "**/*",
    "input": "src/assets",
    "output": "assets"
  },
  "src/manifest.webmanifest"
],
```

In angular.json, a single line was added to the assets array to reference the web manifest file. This line tells the Angular builder to include that file during a build.

app.module.ts

Similarly, app.module.ts had the appropriate references added to import and register the ServiceWorkerModule, pointing at the new configuration file.

```
imports: [
  BrowserModule,
  HttpClientModule,
  IonicModule.forRoot(),
  AppRoutingModule,
  ServiceWorkerModule.register('ngsw-worker.js', {
    enabled: environment.production
  })
],
```

Notice that the service worker is only enabled when `environment.production` is `true`. As a rule, you only want to enable the service worker in production. Otherwise, it may be caching resources and assets you do not want cached while you are developing, and that could cause confusion for yourself or other developers on your team.

That value is managed by two files inside the src/environments folder.

Michael Callaghan

src/environment.ts

```
export const environment = {
  production: false
};
```

src/environment.prod.ts

```
export const environment = {
  production: true
};
```

When you do a production build, the Angular CLI builds the project with the file environment.prod.ts , instead of the non-production environment.ts file.

You can put any environment-specific value inside of the environment object, and then reference that object at run-time. Good Candidates would include URLs to test or staging servers, local assets, and other similar values.

index.html

The last modified file I want to review is index.html.

```
<meta name="apple-mobile-web-app-status-bar-style"
content="black" />
<link rel="manifest" href="manifest.webmanifest">
<meta name="theme-color" content="#75D0F7">
</head>

<body>
  <app-root></app-root>
  <noscript>
    Please enable JavaScript to continue using this
application.
  </noscript>
</body>
```

Michael Callaghan

A link to the web manifest was added to the head section. Remember, the index.html file is the first file the web browser is going to download, so this is how the browser knows where to find your application manifest when needed.

It also added a theme color, fulfilling one of the audit "opportunities." This meta tag will color the address bar and is equivalent to the apple-mobile-web-app-status-bar-style that is already present. This tag applies to non-Apple browsers, such as Chrome and Firefox. Feel free to change the color to any color you like. It is simply an RGB hex color value, the same as you would use in a CSS file.

Finally, there is a new `<noscript>` element inside of the body, immediately after the `<app-root>` component. Recall that one of the audit findings said that you must supply some content if JavaScript is disabled. In browsers without JavaScript enabled, the contents of the `<noscript>` tag will be displayed. You can theoretically put anything in there you want, including alternative page content, images, etc. Though technically this satisfies the audit checklist, it is not an extremely helpful message.

Build and Deploy

Notice, the explanation took a lot more time than adding the @angular/pwa package. Now that you have it, all you need to do it make another production build and redeploy.

```
ng build --prod
firebase deploy
```

Updated Audit

Now that the latest version is deployed, go ahead and run the audit again and see how things have improved.

If you closed the browser, reopen it, and navigate back to the application's home page. Return to the Audit tab of the developer tools and run a new audit. If you still have the

Michael Callaghan

results open from the last time, simply click the + just above the performance score. Then click the Run audits button again.

The Result

Simply adding the @angular/pwa package caused the PWA checklist to go green for all but the apple-touch-icon. That is the bottom one, there.

Caching in Action

When you load the application for the first time, you can look in the Network tab of the Chrome Developer Tools to see that all the resources are loaded from the server. However, the next time you reload the page, and look at the asset (image) requests in the Network tab, you can see that all the emergency calls are now coming from the service worker. This is indicated by the term (ServiceWorker) in the Size column.

Michael Callaghan

Switching back over to the Application tab, the Chrome Developer tools will show you the amount of data stored by your application, along with the quota (or amount of storage allowed).

In this case, you can see that the application is using 163KB of application storage, out of 28GB allowed.

Michael Callaghan

If you want, you can also clear the storage from here by clicking the Clear storage button and run the experiment again.

Michael Callaghan

Service Workers and Offline Mode

One of the most critical benefits of using a service worker is the ability to run an application completely offline.

This means even if there is no network connectivity, your application should continue to run as completely as possible.

Obviously, if your application needs to be online for some functions, those functions will not work, and you will want to be able to degrade your functionality gracefully, and at least let the user know that some features will not be available.

For more information on configuring service workers, see https://angular.io/guide/service-worker-config.

Michael Callaghan

Optional: Caching Data Calls

Although the sample app I have provided does not make any API calls, you should know that you can improve the performance of your PWA by caching some of your data.

Naturally, you need to be conscious about the types of API data you would want to cache. With frequently changing content, freshness is usually more important than application performance. It becomes a delicate balancing act, but I will try to give you some guidelines.

To do this type of caching, you need to add some **dataGroups** to our angular service worker configuration file.

Performance Strategy

Consider this sample service worker configuration in ngsw-config.json.

```json
"dataGroups": [
  {
    "name": "cache-first",
    "urls": ["https://mysite.com/api/static/*"],
    "cacheConfig": {
      "maxSize": 250,
      "maxAge": "30d",
      "strategy": "performance"
    }
  }, {
    "name": "latest",
    "urls": ["https://mysite.com/api/latest"],
    "cacheConfig": {
      "maxSize": 1,
      "maxAge": "1d",
      "timeout": "2s",
      "strategy": "freshness"
    }
  }
]
```

Each data group describes the particular type of data you want to cache, along with how you want the service worker to cache that data. In the above configuration I have created a dataGroup I am naming cache-first. Think of this as static data that does not change very often, if at all. Consider things such as country and state names, ISO codes, reference URLs to external web sites, etc. The URLs all follow the same pattern, which I have specified in the URLs array with the endpoint /api/static. If there are more than one URL pattern, you can easily add more inside of the array.

Beneath that is the cache configuration being defined for this data. This setting instructs the service worker to store no more than 250 values in its cache and hang onto them for no more than 30 days. I can specify any numeric value for the maxAge followed by a character standing for milliseconds, seconds, minutes, hours, or days. You can also combine them. So, if I wanted, I could cache for 30d8h27m6s500u

The final setting is the cache strategy, which can be one of two values: performance or freshness. My theory is that the raw details of most static data will not change very often, so there is no reason to worry about freshness. That is why I am comfortable caching it for so long. In fact, I could cache for a lot longer than I am.

Freshness Strategy

The second data group caches the result of a single service call, which I am calling latest. Imagine that this URL on the API returns the constantly or frequently changing information. The cache configuration is entirely different. I am only ever going to store one result, as that is all I can ever get. I am only willing to hang onto it for a day, and in a production app, even that might be too long.

The strategy is completely the opposite as well. I prefer data freshness to performance. I really want the real one, and only

Michael Callaghan

want to fall back to the cached value if I have no other choice. The timeout value is saying to try to get the real one, and only use the cache value if 2 seconds have elapsed and you still cannot get it. This strategy should only occur when the API is unresponsive, or the network is down.

Admittedly, these values are arbitrary. In a production application, you need to weigh the pros and cons against the various strategies.

Michael Callaghan

Installing a PWA on a Mobile Device

Apple and Google have both added support for installing web apps to the home screen with a native icon, just like the native apps you are used to. All you need is a properly configured web manifest file and some special assets, and you're on your way.

In this chapter, you will see what is required to get a PWA installed on the home screen on both iOS and Android devices.

Let us begin this module by describing the state of PWA support on both Android and iOS

Mobile PWA Support

Take a quick look at the current support for progressive web apps in Android and iOS. Keep In mind, this is where things are as I am producing this book. I presume any changes in this list will be for the better.

Android	*iOS*
Icons in Web Manifest	Icons in HTML <link> tags
Splash screen	Splash screen in HTML <link> tags
Push notifications	No push notifications yet
Prompt to install	Share to add to home screen

When you installed the @angular/pwa package, it added icons to the web manifest automatically. Those icons only work on Android, though. For iOS, you need to add them as link tags inside of our index.html page.

Michael Callaghan

Likewise, with the splash screen, Android will create one for you from your icon images, whereas iOS requires a lot more work.

Android offers far superior support for push notification, while iOS still does not support them at all. Obviously, this could change at any time, but it is the case as I am writing this book.

Chrome, Android's default browser, will offer to install a PWA on your home screen, assuming the app is configured properly. For iOS, the user must take a very specific action to do it.

Custom Application Icon

Before you can install the application on the home screen of any mobile device, you will want a custom application icon. This icon is what users will touch to launch the app. Hopefully it will be unique and memorable.

When you added the @angular/pwa package, you got a default set of icons, a bunch of various sizes of the Angular logo. This is the icon that will appear on the home screen of your mobile device if you choose to install it.

Michael Callaghan

I cannot speak for you, but I do not want my custom app represented by the Angular logo. To make matters worse, iOS devices do not honor the icons listed in the service worker config file.

Not surprisingly, there is a tool that will help generate the assets for the app, at all of the appropriate sizes, and also create the link tags for you. You start by providing a single image, much like you did generating the icons. That tool is called the PWA Asset Generator. It is an npm package, which you can install globally or as a development dependency.

```
npm install -g pwa-asset-generator      # Global
install
npm install -D pwa-asset-generator      # Development
dependency
```

I chose an image I found online that looks like the Mario Kart 8 logo. When you choose your own image, remember that it should be a square PNG, at least 512x512 pixels.

Once you have your image, you can use the PWA Asset Generator to create all the icons. The command is a bit complicated, but not too much. Due to its complexity, I prefer to let npm do the heavy lifting for me.

In the project's package.json file, add the following line to the "scripts" section:

```
"icons": "pwa-asset-generator
src/assets/icons/icon.png src/assets/icons
--icon-only -i src/index.html -m
src/manifest.webmanifest",
```

This command has the following parts, which I will explain in detail below.

Michael Callaghan

Command Part	Explanation
`pwa-asset-generator`	The command
`src/assets/icons/icon.png`	The path to the source image
`src/assets/icons`	The output folder where the icons will be written
`--icon-only`	Generate only application icons
`-i src/index.html`	Specifies the path to index.html
`-m src/manifest.webmanifest`	Specifies the path to the web manifest file

Place the source icon in src/assets/icons, and name it icon.png. Next, to generate the icons, execute the following command:

```
npm run icons
```

Then sit back and wait. The asset generator will automatically connect to Apple web servers to determine the appropriate resolutions. It will then generate the appropriate icon sizes, and then update your index.html and web manifest files. If it encounters any errors, which is unlikely, it will report them in the terminal. On my system, I ended up with a folder full of icons of various sizes.

Michael Callaghan

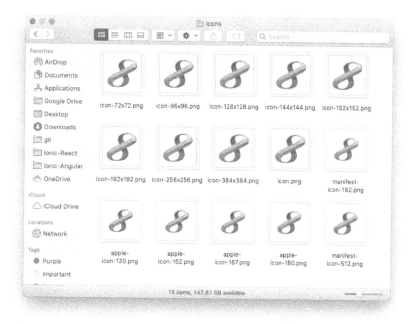

If you want to see what it added to index.html, open the file and look for lines that look like this.

```
<link rel="apple-touch-icon" sizes="180x180"
href="assets/icons/apple-icon-180.png">
<link rel="apple-touch-icon" sizes="167x167"
href="assets/icons/apple-icon-167.png">
<link rel="apple-touch-icon" sizes="152x152"
href="assets/icons/apple-icon-152.png">
<link rel="apple-touch-icon" sizes="120x120"
href="assets/icons/apple-icon-120.png">
```

Notice that all of the icons are not used. That is normal. According to Apple, the icon that is the most appropriate size for the device is used. If there is no icon that matches the recommended size for the device, the smallest icon larger than the recommended size is used. If there are no icons larger than the recommended size, the largest icon is used.

Michael Callaghan

To see these changes, you need to do another production build and deploy.

```
ng build --prod
```

Add PWA to Home Screen

Now that you have an icon, it is time to add the app to the home screen so that it looks like an app.

iOS Add to Home Screen

On iOS devices, the way you do that is to open the URL in Safari. Tap the share icon and choose Add to Home Screen.

You can see the new icon and the name of the app, which you are free to change. You can also see the URL that will be loaded, which cannot be changed.

Click Add, and the icon will be added to your home page.

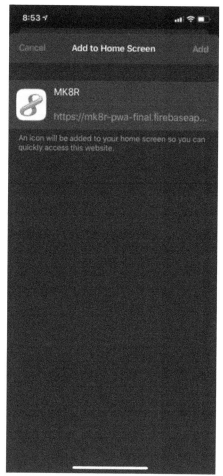
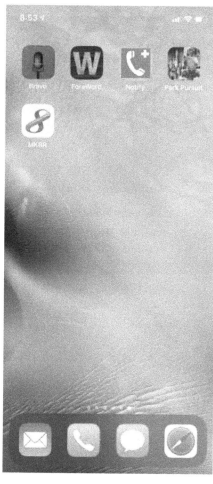

Michael Callaghan

Android Add to Home Screen

On Android, things are a little different. If your application is deemed "worthy" by Chrome, then it will automatically offer

to add the app to the home screen. In this case, worthy does not mean that it can lift Thor's hammer. It means that it is configured as a proper PWA, which by now, the Mario Kart Randomizer most certainly is. Here is an example of Chrome on a Galaxy S7 determining that the app is worthy to be installed.

If you close the toast message, or click Cancel on the confirmation alert, Chrome will not ask again for some period of time Google specifies, depending on how often the app is run. Some of the information I have seen indicates that it could take up to 3 months. Fortunately, there is also a manual method, which is similar to the iOS method.

Click the Chrome menu and choose Add to Home Screen. Chrome will ask you to confirm your choice. Once you do, the app's icon will be placed in its appropriate spot with the rest of the apps. It can then be opened just like any other app.

Michael Callaghan

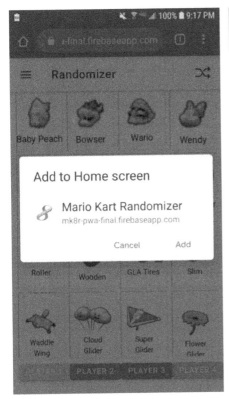
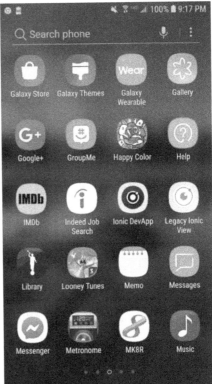

Michael Callaghan

Custom Splash Screen

You have probably noticed that most, if not all, mobile apps start up by briefly showing a screen of non-interactive content. Almost everyone refers to this as a splash screen. Apple, of course, has to be different, calling it a startup image or a launch screen. And as you may have guessed by now, iOS devices have a special way of specifying a custom one for a PWA.

Android Splash Screen Guidelines

On Android, if you have configured your PWA properly (and yes, you already have), most of the work is done for you. Android devices will automatically provide a splash screen as long you adhere to four simple rules:

1. The name property is set to the name of your PWA.

2. The background_color property is set to a valid CSS color value.

3. The icons array specifies an icon that is at least 512px by 512px.

4. The icon exists and is a PNG.

The splash screen it generates is based on the icon.

Michael Callaghan

iOS Splash Screen Guidelines

Of course, here again, Apple is different. Shown below are three of my apps being launched on an iPhone. Each one is an Ionic/Angular app, but the first two were built with

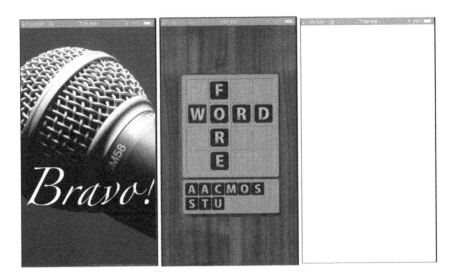

Cordova to generate the iOS-specific version.

Notice that each one of them has an attractive and brief splash screen. MK8R, on the other hand, shows a white screen. Fortunately, it is possible to fix. We will use the same PWA Asset Generator we used to generate the icons.

Although you can reuse the icon image used to generate the splash screens, that is not strictly necessary. What the image is turns out to be less important than the physical characteristics of the image. Use any tool you like to create it, but you need to make sure it fits the following criteria:

- Though other formats may work, everything I have read indicates that it should be a PNG file.

Michael Callaghan

- You need to provide the appropriate sizes for the various iOS devices your app will target.

- Because not all of the screen sizes are exactly the same proportions, it helps if you keep your important content centered.

- To that end, apple recommends that you do not put any text on the image at all. I usually have the app name but remember that it will not be translated into other languages.

The most common pattern I have seen is to make it look like your app's icon, which is what I recommend. Once you have your images, you need to add the appropriate tags to the index.html page.

Generate the Splash Screens

Add another line to the "scripts" section in package.json. It is similar to the one you added for the icons, so it should be very familiar.

```
"splash": "pwa-asset-generator
src/assets/icons/icon.png src/assets/splash --
splash-only -i src/index.html",
```

This command has the following parts, which I will explain in detail below.

Command Part	Explanation
pwa-asset-generator	The command
src/assets/icons/ico n.png	The path to the source image
src/assets/splash	The output folder where the splash screens will be written

Michael Callaghan

`--splash-only`	Generate only splash screens
`-i src/index.html`	Specifies the path to index.html

Generate the splash screens by executing the following command:

```
npm run splash
```

Then sit back and wait. As before, the asset generator will automatically connect to Apple web servers to determine the appropriate resolutions. It will then generate the appropriate icon sizes, and then update your index.html.

These splash screens are only relevant to iOS, so the only changes need to be made to index.html, and not to the web manifest files.

If it encounters any errors, which is unlikely, it will report them in the terminal. On my system, I ended up with a folder full of splash screens of various sizes.

Finally, you can do another production build and deploy.

And with that, once the application has updated, you can close it quickly, and then open it back up.

If you did everything right, you see the new splash screen. The iOS version is the one you generated, and on Android the one that was generated automatically by the system.

Michael Callaghan

Application Updates

A major benefit of service workers is the ability to download and apply updates automatically. The @angular/pwa package provides the SwUpdate service to make updating your application quick and painless. There are two relevant observables you can subscribe to, and one function to call.

SwUpdate Member	Explanation
available	Indicates that the service worker has determined that there are pending updates to the application. These updates will be installed as soon as the application is reloaded.
activated	Indicates that the service worker is now serving the new version.
checkForUpdates	Enables you to check for updates manually, which you would typically only need to do in a long-running application.

Updates Available

The SwUpdate object provides an **available** observable that you can subscribe to. It will fire whenever the service worker has determined a new version of the application is available.

In the following code, I am subscribing to the observable by passing the entire event to another function on the component called **onUpdateAvailable**.

```
private updater: SwUpdate
   . . .
```

Michael Callaghan

```
this.updater
.available
.subscribe(event =>
this.onUpdateAvailable(event));
. . .
onUpdateAvailable(event: UpdateAvailableEvent)
```

The parameter event being passed to the function, is of the type `UpdateAvailableEvent`, an interface containing information about the update. Here is the definition of that interface.

```
export interface UpdateAvailableEvent {
  type: 'UPDATE_AVAILABLE';
  current: {
    hash: string;
    appData?: Object;
  };
  available: {
    hash: string;
    appData?: Object;
  };
}
```

It contains information about the current version, as well as the available version. The `appData` refers to a user-defined object loaded from the ngsw-config file, and can contain just about anything you want to include. You can use it to provide information about the new version, sort of like a change log.

Update Activated

The `SwUpdate` object also provides an observable called `activated`. It will fire when the new version is activated. In this code, I am subscribing to the observable by passing the entire event to another function on the component called `onUpdateAvailable`.

Michael Callaghan

```
private updater: SwUpdate
  . . .
  this.updater
  .activated
  .subscribe(() => this.onUpdateActivated());
  . . .
onUpdateActivated(event: UpdateActivatedEvent)
```

The parameter event being passed to the function, is of the
type UpdateActivatedEvent. It is also an interface containing
information about the update. It is almost identical to the
UpdateAvailableEvent interface.

In reality, I have not found much use for this event. The only
time I have ever seen it fire is during a manual update
activation.

Manually Check for Updates

Normally, the SwUpdater works silently in the background,
based on the running service worker. However, the service
worker only checks for updates on application launch. If you
have a long-running application, there is a function you can
call from inside your own code to check for updates at a time
you choose. This can be done on a timer, or in response to a
user action.

Check for Update Function

Shown here is a function that you can call whenever you want
to check for updates.

```
async checkForUpdate() {
  if (this.updater.isEnabled) {
    console.log('Checking for updates...');
    await this.updater.checkForUpdate();
  }
}
```

We have seen a version of this function before, so it should
look familiar. It first ensures that the updater is enabled. If it

Michael Callaghan

is, it will display a toast message indicating that it is checking for updates.

If the updated is not enabled, it will display a toast indicating that.

Curiously, there really is no way for you to find out the result of the checkForUpdate call. If there is a pending update, the available event will fire. If not, nothing will happen. That may be why I think Angular suggests doing it on a timer as your first choice.

Michael Callaghan

Implementing Updates in MK8R

Now I will show you how to implement application updates in your own application, by adding it to the MK8R sample application.

On the UI side, you will make use of a couple of handy Ionic components.

The Ionic `AlertController` provides you a means of quickly getting user confirmation of whether to proceed with an action. You will use that to ask permission to update the application.

The Ionic `ToastController` lets you present a small and brief popup (or toast) message. You will use that when the application has been updated to a new version.

Updates Available

When you receive a notice of a pending update, the polite thing to do is ask the user of your application whether or not they want to update it now or wait until the next time the app is launched. One way to do that is with an Ionic `AlertController`, shown here.

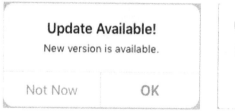
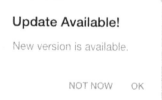

Everything you need to generate a brief message to the user can be done with this handy utility. All of the styling and user interface are handled for you, though you can control most of it. As with every other Ionic component, this one styles itself

Michael Callaghan

depending on your browser. The example shown above on the left is how the alert will look on iOS devices. The one on the right is the Material Design version, shown on non-iOS devices and desktop browsers.

Here is my function to handle the **updatesAvailable** event.

```
async onUpdatesAvailable(event:
UpdateAvailableEvent) {
    const alert = await this.alertController
      .create({
        header: 'Update Available!',
        message: 'New version is available.'
          +
event.available.appData['updateMessage'],
        buttons: [
          {
            text: 'Later',
            role: 'cancel'
          }, {
            text: 'Now',
            handler: async () => {
              await this.updater.activateUpdate();
              window.location.reload();
            }
          }
        ]
      });
    alert.present();
  }
```

In this version, a new **alertController** is created with a header, or title, that says "Update Available."

The next line is the body of the alert, a string saying that a new version is available. It also includes **appData** information from the event parameter, describing what is in the update. For now, it is simply a generic message. I will show you how to customize that a bit later.

Below that are two buttons, one labeled "Later" and the other labeled "Now." The "Later" button has a role of cancel, which means on a desktop browser, pressing the Escape key will cause it to be selected, and the alert dismissed. Because of the cancel role, this button does not need a handler, unless you were to want to take another action.

The "Now" button has a handler defined completely in line with an asynchronous arrow function. If the user clicks the "Now" button, the code calls the activateUpdate function on the SwUpdater object, waits for it to finish, and then forces the browser window to reload. The handler shown here for the OK button is right out of Angular's own documentation.

All of this code is passed as an options object to the create function and stored in the alert variable. The create function returns a promise, which means it needs to be awaited. Even then, though, nothing actually gets displayed until you call the alert object's present function. The application blocks at that point, forcing the user to take one of the provided actions.

Subscribe to the Event

The alert code above will not do any good if you do not also subscribe to the event. You can do that inside the initializeApp function in the same file. Simply add the following line to the function.

```
this.updater.available.subscribe({
    next: (event) =>
this.onUpdatesAvailable(event) });
```

Recall that SwUpdate.available is an Observable, so you need to subscribe to it. The code above will call the supplied function, onUpdatesAvailable, every time the service worker detects that a new update is available.

Inform the User the Update Is Finished

The Toast Controller is another Ionic component you can use to provide your users with a subtle notification that something has occurred. In this case, MK8R will show a brief toast message when the application has been updated to the new version.

Add the following code into app.component.ts. It will display a Toast message with whatever message is provided.

```
async showToastMessage(msg: string) {
   const toast = await
this.toastController.create({
      message: msg,
      duration: 2000,
      position: 'top',
      buttons: [
        {
          text: 'Close',
          role: 'cancel'
        }
      ]
   });
   toast.present();
}
```

Displaying a Toast message is very similar to displaying an Alert. The primary difference is that there is no choice for the user to make. You start by calling the Toast Controller's create function, passing an object of options. There are lots of options to choose from, with the most common being displayed here.

The most important is the message you want to display to the user, controlled by the message field. Here I am setting its value to the msg parameter passed to the function.

The next field, duration, determines the number of milliseconds the toast will remain visible. In this case, it is 2 seconds. If you omit this, the toast will remain visible until dismissed, either by the user or by calling its dismiss function. I recommend always setting a duration.

Michael Callaghan

The `position` field is a string that can be set to **top**, **middle**, or **bottom**. The toast will be horizontally centered on the window, vertically positioned depending on the value of this field. The default is to position toast at the bottom of the window.

The `buttons` array defines one or more buttons to be displayed inside the toast next to the `message`. You can see I am providing a single button, **Close**, with the role of `cancel`. This works exactly the same as the cancel button in the Alert Controller.

The create function, as expected, returns a promise, so you will await it. The promise resolves to a toast object, which you can then use to call present. Present also returns a promise, but there is no need to wait for it to resolve. There is, of course, more you can do with the Toast. For more details, see the official Ionic docs.

Subscribe to the Event

Just as we saw before, the toast code above requires you to subscribe to the appropriate event. You can also do that inside the `initializeApp` function in the same file. Simply add the following line to the function.

```
this.updater.activated.subscribe({
     next: () => this.showToastMessage('App
updated.') });
```

Recall that `SwUpdate.activated` is an Observable, so you need to subscribe to it. The code above will call the supplied function, `showToastMessage`, every time the service worker detects that a new update has been applied.

Manually Check for Updates

If your application is one that runs for long periods of time, it might make sense to check for updates periodically, or provide a way for the user to check. The techniques are similar, so I will show you a simple way to implement a menu item to check for updates on demand.

Ask for Pending Updates

This function is similar to the one you saw before. Place it in the component class inside app.component.ts.

```
async checkForUpdate() {
  if (this.updater.isEnabled) {
    this.showToastMessage('Checking for
updates...');
    await this.updater.checkForUpdate();
  }
}
```

As you can see, it is reusing the toast message to provide some user feedback, instead of writing to the console log where it would likely go unnoticed.

Check for Update User Interface

Now open app.component.html and look for the `<ion-menu>` code. This is where the side menu is defined. Edit this file to look like this:

```
<ion-app>
  <ion-split-pane contentId="main-content">
    <ion-menu contentId="main-content"
type="overlay">
      <ion-header>
        <ion-toolbar>
          <ion-title>Menu</ion-title>
        </ion-toolbar>
      </ion-header>
      <ion-content>
        <ion-list>
          <ion-menu-toggle auto-hide="false"
                *ngFor="let p of appPages">
            <ion-item [routerDirection]="'root'"
                [routerLink]="[p.url]">
              <ion-icon slot="start"
[name]="p.icon"></ion-icon>
```

```
            <ion-label>
              {{p.title}}
            </ion-label>
          </ion-item>
        </ion-menu-toggle>
        <ion-menu-toggle auto-hide="false">
          <ion-item button
(click)="checkForUpdate()"
            detail="false"
[disabled]="!updater.isEnabled">
            <ion-icon slot="start" name="cloud-
download"></ion-icon>
            <ion-label>Check for Update
              <span *ngIf="!updater.isEnabled">
Unavailable</span>
            </ion-label>
          </ion-item>
        </ion-menu-toggle>
      </ion-list>
    </ion-content>
  </ion-menu>
  <ion-router-outlet id="main-content"></ion-
router-outlet>
  </ion-split-pane>
</ion-app>
```

The highlighted lines are the new code to be added.
Everything else is for context.

The new menu item starts with an `<ion-menu-toggle>`. If
you want an item in your menu to close the menu when you
select it, be sure to wrap it with an `<ion-menu-toggle>`
component. Otherwise, the menu will stay open.

The `<ion-menu-toggle>` can also be used to open a menu
(hence the name toggle). By default, it will automatically hide
itself whenever it detects that its menu is disabled or being
presented in an `<ion-split-pane>`, as is the case here.
Because of that, if you want it to be visible all the time, be
sure to set its **auto-hide** attribute to **false**. I will not reveal

Michael Callaghan

me how long it took me to debug that the first time I forgot it.

Inside the toggle is an `<ion-item>` with a `button` attribute and a `click` handler. The button attribute is a hint that adds an animation to the click effect. In other words, it will look and act like the rest of the menu items.

The `click` handler is defined to call the `checkForUpdate` function on the component, which you have already seen. Make sure you get the binding syntax right, as shown here. Otherwise, you could end up with nothing happening when a user clicks the menu.

The `disabled` attribute is set to an expression that will evaluate to `true` if the `updater` is not enabled. Note the square brackets, indicating that Angular should evaluate the expression rather than use it as-is.

The attribute `detail="false"` will prevent the menu from having a gray forward chevron on its side. It makes sense for the menu items that navigate to other pages but does not really work for a command like this.

If you want to customize that visible line separating the menu items, add a `lines` attribute with the value to `full` or `none`.

Inside the `<ion-item>` is an `<ion-icon>` with its `slot` set to `start` and its `name` set to `cloud-download`. Again, pay attention to the binding syntax.

The `<ion-label>` next to the icon defines the text to be displayed. Inside of the label is an HTML `<span>` with an `*ngIf` directive. The expression in the directive will ensure that the word "Unavailable" is only displayed when the `updater` is not enabled.

Build and Deploy

To get these changes deployed, add two more lines to the scripts section in package.json.

Michael Callaghan

```
"prod": "ng build --prod",
"postprod": "firebase deploy"
```

These two scripts will make it easier to deploy the application. They are the same two commands seen throughout this book. The difference is that now they can be run more or less automatically.

To build and deploy the app, simply type the command

```
npm run prod
```

The npm system will run the script defined as prod, and if successful, run any script also named "prod" but prepended with "post." It is a minor shortcut, I admit, but these things can add up.

Run that command now and then open a browser to the Firebase URL provided. Next, I will show you how to force an update.

Complete app.component.ts File

The complete app.component.html file is provided above. Below is the complete source code listing for app.components.ts. These two files represent all of the changes needed to get the application updates working. Given all the functionality enabled by @angular/pwa, it is amazing that no code changes were required until this point.

```
import { Component } from '@angular/core';

import { Platform, AlertController, ToastController
} from '@ionic/angular';
import { SwUpdate, UpdateAvailableEvent } from
'@angular/service-worker';

@Component({
```

```
  selector: 'app-root',
  templateUrl: 'app.component.html',
  styleUrls: ['app.component.scss']
})
export class AppComponent {
  public appPages = [
    {
      title: 'Home',
      url: '/home',
      icon: 'home'
    },
    {
      title: 'Randomizer',
      url: '/slots',
      icon: 'shuffle'
    },
    {
      title: 'Settings',
      url: '/settings',
      icon: 'settings'
    }
  ];

  constructor(
    private alertController: AlertController,
    private platform: Platform,
    private toastController: ToastController,
    public updater: SwUpdate

  ) {
    this.initializeApp();
  }

  initializeApp() {
    this.platform.ready().then(() => { });
    this.updater.available.subscribe({ next: (event)
=> this.onUpdatesAvailable(event) });
    this.updater.activated.subscribe({ next: () =>
this.showToastMessage('App updated.') });
  }

  async onUpdatesAvailable(event:
UpdateAvailableEvent) {
```

Michael Callaghan

```
      const alert = await this.alertController
        .create({
          header: 'Update Available!',
          message: 'New version is available.' +
  event.available.appData['updateMessage'],
          buttons: [
            {
              text: 'Later',
              role: 'cancel'
            }, {
              text: 'Now',
              handler: async () => {
                await this.updater.activateUpdate();
                window.location.reload();
              }
            }
          ]
        });
      alert.present();
  }


  async showToastMessage(msg: string) {
    const toast = await
  this.toastController.create({
      message: msg,
      duration: 2000,
      position: 'top',
      buttons: [
        {
          text: 'Close',
          role: 'cancel'
        }
      ]
    });
    toast.present();
  }

  async checkForUpdate() {
    if (this.updater.isEnabled) {
      this.showToastMessage('Checking for
  updates...');
      await this.updater.checkForUpdate();
```

Michael Callaghan

```
    } else {
      this.showToastMessage('Updates are not
enabled.')
    }
  }
}
```

Michael Callaghan

Updates in Action

Now that the update code is deployed, you probably want to see it work. The easy solution is to make any change to the application and then deploy it. Testing both the manual and automatic detection might take a little more planning, which is what this chapter is for.

Updating your app involves the following distinct steps:

1. Modify the application.

2. Update the version information.

3. Provide an update message.

4. Build and deploy the updated application.

Technically, step 1 is not necessary. Any change to any file in the application will cause the service worker to determine the application has changed. So that is what I will show you how to do. I presume you know how to change the application itself.

Test Automatic Update

To test the automatic update, make the following two changes now.

1. Open package.json and change the value of `version`.

2. Open ngsw-config.json and add the following block of code immediately after the line `"index"`:

```
    "/index.html",
  "appData": {
    "updateMessage": "We added a whiz-bang new
feature!"
  },
```

Michael Callaghan

The object specified by `appData` will be passed into the `UpdateAvailableEvent`, which will then be parsed and displayed inside the `onUpdatesAvailable` function.

Next, run a build and deploy with the command.

```
npm run prod
```

Once it has deployed, open a browser to the Firebase URL. Shortly after the application loads, it should present the Update Available alert. If you choose "Later," it should still download the new assets, but not reload the window. If you choose "Now," the application will update, the window will reload automatically, the `activated` event should fire, and the toast notification displayed.

Test Manual Update

To test the manual update feature, you need to leave the application running, make a change similar to one you just did, rebuild, and then deploy. I recommend again changing the version, and then editing the `appData.updateMessage` to be something a little different.

With the application still running, build and deploy the application. Once deployed, simply open the menu and select the Check for Update item.

The rest of the update experience should be the same.

How Does the Service Worker Know a New Version is Available?

Have you wondered yet how the service worker knows there is a new version of your app?

At build time, the Angular CLI will use the information in the ngsw-config.json file to generate another file, ngsw.json. The latter file is part of your web site and is deployed alongside the rest of your application. It contains the complete list of all files matching the patterns specified in the ngsw-config.json file.

In the example shown here, the *.js pattern on the left was expanded to match every generated .js file.

ngsw-config.json	ngsw.json
| ```
"assetGroups": [
{
    "name": "app",
    "installMode":
    "prefetch",
    "resources": {
        "files": [
            "/fav
            icon.
            ico",
            "/ind
            ex.ht
            ml",
            "/*.c
            ss",
            "/*.j
            s",
            "/svg
            /**"
        ]
    }
}
``` | ```
"assetGroups": [
{
    "name": "app",
    "installMode": "prefetc
    h",
    "updateMode": "prefetch
    ",
    "urls": [
        "/1.5ee61653062cd9
        3abb29.js",
        "/100.04fee9894126
        d6d4b4b2.js",
        "/101.c29059f5ed90
        db678b90.js",
        . . .
    ]
}, "hashTable": {
    "/1.5ee61653062cd93abb2
    9.js": "...",
    "/100.04fee9894126d6d4b
    4b2.js": "...",
    "/101.c29059f5ed90db678
    b90.js": "...",
``` |

When the service worker starts up, it loads the contents of ngsw.json and immediately begins to process it. Any assets listed as **prefetch** will be quietly downloaded in the background.

A significant portion of the ngsw.json file is the hashTable section, which contains a hash value of each of these files expanded above.

Michael Callaghan

Any time ngsw.json changes, or any of the file hash values change, the service worker knows that there is a new version of the application available. The change can be anything: an image, a script file, an html page, or even a single character in a style sheet.

Michael Callaghan

Final Considerations

I hope you enjoyed this book as much as I enjoyed creating it, and that you have enough information to go and implement your own PWA and share them with me and the world.

There are a few other considerations I want to share with you. Consider it food for thought, and maybe some next steps you can take.

Push Notification

Implementing push notification is the next big thing in the PWA world, and should be your next big step for your own apps. I really wanted to include push notification in this book, and saved it for the final module in the hopes it would be ready to implement. The SwPush object is actually included with the service worker and part of the @angular/pwa package you use in the book. The problem was the inconsistent support between web, Android, and iPhone. Plus getting it working from the server, both when the app is running and when it is not, was simply too flaky for comfort.

Michael Callaghan

I am sure the support will continue to improve rapidly. Keep watching the Angular docs at https://angular.io/api/service-worker/SwPush.

Trusted Web Activities

Did you know that Google is starting to allow PWAs to be packaged for the Play Store? It is called a Trusted Web Activity, and is a way to deploy your PWA as an Android app.

Granted, if you are using Ionic already, it probably makes more sense to use Cordova and let that do the heavy lifting for you. That said, it is good to know there are options.

You read more about Trusted Web Activities at https://developers.google.com/web/android/trusted-web-activity.

Michael Callaghan

Capacitor

Another way to enhance your PWA with native capabilities is to use Capacitor, a cross-platform bridge from the folks who brought you Ionic. If you need native functionality that is not otherwise available, Capacitor can probably get you what you need, with a lower learning curve than Cordova.

Learn more at https://capacitor.ionicframework.com.

Appscope

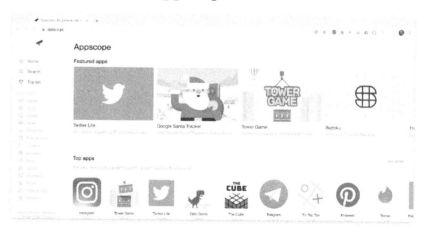

Michael Callaghan

When you're ready to show off your PWA to the world, you can add it to the growing list of amazing PWAs at Appscope: https://appsco.pe/

Google Lighthouse

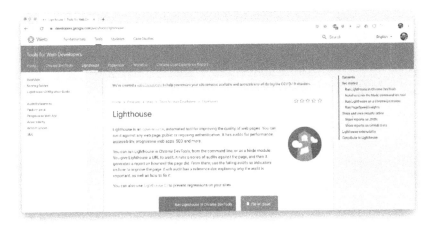

As you continue working with PWAs, don't forget to check your app with Lighthouse. If you'd like more information on using it, visit the lighthouse page at developers.google.com.

Twitter

Michael Callaghan

And please follow me and share your PWAs and feedback on Twitter. My handle is @walkingriver. Use the hashtags #PWA and #BetOnTheWeb

Online Video Courses

Finally, I would be delighted if you check out my Ionic courses, those on Pluralsight and on my own hosted site.

Pluralsight: https://bit.ly/ps-mike

CourseCraft: https://coursecraft.net/users/cREs

As a special reward for completing this book, I am pleased to offer you a 50% discount on any of my CourseCraft courses. Simply enroll in any (or all) of my classes using the promo code I have hidden in this book. Hint: It is the `theme_color` value in the web manifest file without the # sign.

Let me know what you think, and what you would like to see me work on next for my next book or course. There is also a handy place for subscribers to ask questions.

Thank you for reading this book on Developing Progressive Web Apps with Angular (and Ionic).

Now go out and create something amazing!

Michael Callaghan

Appendix: Hardware and Software Requirements

One of the great advantages to using cross-platform tools and frameworks is that you have so many choices of hardware and OS combinations that you can choose. It is also one of the primary disadvantages. I will try to cover the simplest combinations to help get you up and running quickly.

The tools I use in this book run on any modern OS: You should be able to follow along on a Mac, Linux, or Windows. I will be using mostly macOS. If you do not have a Mac, you should still be able to do everything I cover.

Code Editor

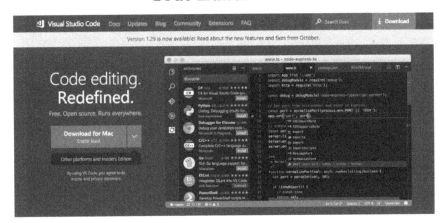

For my code samples, I will be using Microsoft Visual Studio Code exclusively. VS Code is a free and open source and cross-platform development environment, designed from the ground up to work with the technologies you will be using.

You are, of course, free to use whichever editor or IDE you are comfortable with.

Michael Callaghan

If you want to try VS Code, simply visit
https://code.visualstudio.com, click the big green download
button, and install.

Command Line Tooling

As I said, Angular and Ionic and their tooling support a wide
variety of desktop platforms. You will need to ensure you
have all the other tools installed before you can start.

- NodeJS
- NPM
- Git

Most of the tools you will use rely on NodeJS, a JavaScript-
based runtime environment.

NPM is a package manager built on top of node. Most of our
tools are deployed as npm packages. It is installed with node.

To download the sample app, you will be using Git, a
powerful and flexible source control system, and its related
tools. If you have a Mac or Linux, you probably already have
it.

Quite frankly, that is about it. Installing these items depends
on your platform.

Windows Quick Start

If you are on Windows, this section should get you up and
running as quickly as possible. I am going to assume you do
not have any of the following tools. If you do, please just skip
that step.

Git

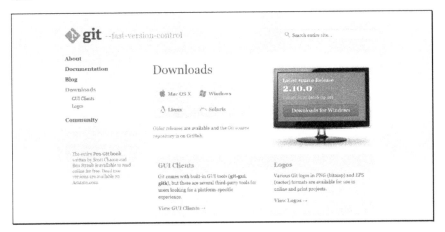

First, you will need the latest version of Git. Depending on your code editor or IDE of choice, it is possible to avoid typing most git commands.

Git for Windows installs an alternative command prompt, called Git Bash. I recommend using that over the windows command prompt wherever possible.

You should be able to click the Downloads for Windows button, select the default for your system (probably the 64-bit Git for Windows, and then install with the default options.

Node

Next, you will need to have NodeJS, which will become the foundation of everything you do in this book.

The most straightforward method is downloading and installing it right from nodejs.org. It is quick and painless. The only real drawback is that it limits you to only one version of Node being installed at a time. Believe it or not, that can be a real problem for some developers, who support multiple apps, each built on a different version of Node. It will not be a problem for this book, so you are safe in installing from here.

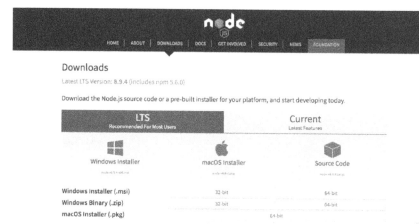

Visit https://nodejs.org. You will want to download the latest LTS (or long-term support) version of Node.

Once downloaded, simply run the installer. Accepting the installer's defaults should get you what you need.

macOS Quick Start

If you use a Mac, this section will show you how to install the tools you are going to need. If you are not using a Mac, feel free to skip ahead to the next section.

Homebrew

On a Mac, most of the tools you need to install can be installed through Homebrew. Homebrew bills itself as the Mac's missing package manager.

Michael Callaghan

There are a lot of tools and runtime packages available through Homebrew, so I recommend installing it if you do not already have it. You can install it by copying and pasting the following command into any terminal window.

```
/bin/bash -c "$(curl -fsSL
https://raw.githubusercontent.com/Homebrew/install/m
aster/install.sh)"
```

Git

Next you should install Git. But first, check to see if you have it.

 In a terminal window, enter the command

```
git --version
```

If it is installed, you will see a version number, probably 2.x or something. If you have a version that says, "Apple Git", it means you installed it through the XCode command line tools. This should be ok.

If you do not have git, and you installed Homebrew, simply issue the command

Michael Callaghan

```
brew install git
```

This will give you the latest version for your system.

If you prefer to install git from the official site, you can do that, too. Head over to https://git-scm.com, click the download button, and follow the instructions.

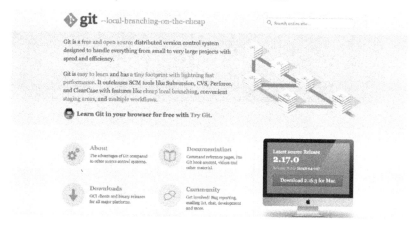

Node

Next, tackle node. There are three ways to install node. Each is valid and has its own positives and negatives. I will try to give you enough information for you to make an intelligent

choice. Review them and choose the one you prefer.

Michael Callaghan

If you like installing items from their source, feel free to head over to https://nodejs.org and click the big green button. The tools you are going to be using require at least Node 8, so you should not have any issues here. I recommend downloading and installing the LTS, or long-term-support version.

Node (Homebrew)

You can also use Homebrew to install node. Simply enter the command

```
brew install node
```

in a terminal window.

While it is installing, I would like to point out a few things that you will be seeing. The first thing Homebrew tries to do is update its local indexes. This is how it knows what software is available. The massive amount of text that fills the screen are all the new or updated software packages that Homebrew has been found since the last time it was run on this system.

Homebrew then finds node and its dependencies. It continues to download and install the dependencies, and finally, it installs node itself.

After not too long, depending on your internet connection, node is installed.

Note that the version of Node that gets installed is Node 12, which as of this writing, is the latest version available. You could have changed the brew command to specify a different version. And you are still stuck with just a single version of node, which may or may not be what you need all the time.

Fortunately, there is a better way, which I describe in detail in Node Version Manager.

Michael Callaghan

Linux Quick Start

If you plan to follow along on Linux, the tools should be straightforward

These steps were tested on Ubuntu Desktop 18.10, Cosmic Cuttlefish, which uses Debian packages. If you use a different version of Linux, you will need to alter these steps to work with your distribution's package manager.

There are two things you need to install: Node and Git.

There are three ways to install node. Each is valid and has its own its own positives and negatives. I will try to give you enough information for you to make an intelligent choice. Review them and choose the one you prefer.

The first method is to download directly from nodejs.org itself. Quite frankly, I do not recommend this method. However, if you like installing items from their official locations, feel free to head over to https://nodejs.org and click the big green button. I recommend downloading and installing the LTS, or long-term-support version.

Another way is to install node from the Ubuntu command line. Open a terminal window and type

```
node --version
```

Michael Callaghan

to see if you already have it. In my pristine system, I do not. But Ubuntu tells me exactly how to get it.

To install it, simply enter the command provided, which should be

```
sudo apt-get install node
```

and it gets installed.

Now when you type node --version, you should see that the default Ubuntu version was installed. In my case, I got 8.10. So that is the second way, and it is better than the first, though you probably are not getting the LTS version. Fortunately, there is a third method, which is far more flexible. I describe that in the next section.

Node Version Manager

Now let us review another way to install Node on macOS and Linux. My preferred approach to anything relating to node and npm is to install a tool called the Node Version Manager, or nvm. It is a little more involved, but far more flexible in the long run.

What is nvm? It is an elegant set of shell script functions to enable the most flexible use of node imaginable.

The primary purpose of nvm is to enable you to install and switch between multiple versions of node and npm instantly. So, if you happen to have one project that requires Node 8, but another one that requires Node 4, for example, it is easy to keep them both installed, yet still independent from one another.

To me, the more important features of nvm revolve around root, or administrator access. Many npm package installation instructions you will find on the web instruct you to use the sudo (or super-user do) command to install packages globally. It is possible that you may not have root access to your Mac, making those instructions worthless. There are workarounds,

Michael Callaghan

naturally, and they work fine. I used such workarounds for a few years before a colleague showed me nvm. Now I am convinced.

Once you commit to nvm, there is no reason ever to use sudo. In fact, you do not even need root access to install nvm. Everything gets installed under your own user account.

On macOS, install nvm with this command. It uses Homebrew, which you should now have.

```
brew install nvm
```

If you are on Linux, use this command, as these tools should exist on a stock Linux system.

```
wget -qO- https://raw.githubusercontent.com/nvm-sh/nvm/v0.35.3/install.sh | bash
```

One you have installed nvm, you can use it to install any version of node that you want. In this case, you will install the latest stable version. Simply execute the commands shown here.

Command	Description
nvm install 'lts/*'	Download and install the latest long-term-support, or LTS, version of Node.
node --version nvm current	Determine which version of node is currently in use.
nvm ls	Determine which versions of node you have installed
nvm ls-remote	Determine what versions of node are available to you. Warning: It is a pretty long list.

Michael Callaghan

`nvm install v10.15`	Install any available version of node (the v is optional).
`nvm use v12.4`	Switch to another version of nvm you have installed (the v is optional)

From this point forward, all of node and every npm package you install globally will be placed in the .nvm directory inside of your home directory. You should never have to use sudo to install an npm package globally. You're welcome.

www.ingramcontent.com/pod-product-compliance
Lightning Source LLC
Chambersburg PA
CBHW031245050326
40690CB00007B/965